The
Princess Dessert
Cookbook

Desserts Inspired by Disney, Star Wars,
Classic Fairy Tales, Real-Life Princesses, and More!

The Princess Dessert Cookbook

Desserts Inspired by Disney, Star Wars, Classic Fairy Tales, Real-Life Princesses, and More!

AURÉLIA BEAUPOMMIER

Photography: Amandine Honegger
Styling: Sylvie Rost
Translation: Grace McQuillan

Skyhorse Publishing

Author's Note

Every occasion—an afternoon snack, birthday, family get-together, or holiday—is the perfect excuse to concoct a delicious dessert.... Whether you're alone in the kitchen or with your children, I want you to *enjoy* beating egg whites into peaks, watching choux pastry rise, and baking a sponge cake to the most beautiful golden brown!

Princesses (and princes!) are to fairy tales what chocolate is to dessert—essential! And like chocolate, they can either go for a classic look or a bit of modern flair. The princesses and princes mentioned in this book have been carefully chosen by my own personal princesses—who are very much with the times—and you won't find a single limp marshmallow among them: each and every one has quite a personality!

If by an unfortunate spell you happen to have a food intolerance or allergy, not to worry—most of the recipes in this book contain substitution ingredients so everyone can enjoy dessert as it should be.

It is with great pleasure that I share our favorite recipes with you. These are the ones that make little eyes shine and little mouths say things like, "So good!" "More, please!" and, "Will there be any left for snack tomorrow?"

These princess (and prince!) desserts are the result of wonderful moments spent with people I love. I hope with all my heart that it will be the same for you. Special desserts to make with the whole family . . . I don't think there's anything better!

Aurélia Beaupommier

This book is for my daughters, Emily and Héloïse.

Who am I?

Aurélia Beaupommier is a passionate reader of magic and fantasy literature. After falling into a cauldron filled with apples, musketeers, magicians, and great explorers one day, she decided to join the French National Center for Scientific Research, where she worked for many years as a librarian. As enthusiastic about reading as she is about cooking, she now lives with her family in Normandy in a secret place where there are "books, friends, and flowers" and where she created these recipes inspired by princes and princesses.

Contents

The Author's Golden Recipe

A Birthday Cake for My Princesses: Chocolate Cloud

SERVES 8 DESSERT LOVERS

Preparation: 20 minutes

Cooking: 40 minutes

7 ounces (200 grams) dark baking chocolate

6 ounces (180 grams) butter

6 eggs

1¾ ounces (50 grams) flour

1¾ ounces (50 grams) cornstarch

1 teaspoon (5½ grams) baking powder

6 ounces (180 grams) granulated sugar

1 packet Smarties® or other sugar-coated chocolate candy for decoration

Salt

Prepare a water bath by placing an empty saucepan over another saucepan filled halfway with water. Begin heating.

Break the chocolate into pieces, slice the butter, and put both into the empty saucepan to melt.

Preheat the oven to 350°F (180°C, th.6).

Crack the eggs and separate the whites from the yolks.

Sift the flour, cornstarch, and baking powder over a bowl. Then add the sugar and the egg yolks, one at a time.

Sprinkle a pinch of salt over the egg whites and use a mixer to beat them into stiff peaks: beat slowly at first, then faster and faster. The whites are perfect if nothing falls out when you turn the bowl over.

Pour the chocolate-butter mixture into the flour–egg yolk mixture a little at a time. This will prevent the heat from cooking the eggs. Next, add the beaten egg whites.

Transfer the mixture to your favorite cake mold and bake for around 40 minutes.

Let cool and decorate with Smarties®—let your imagination guide you.

This rich and incredibly moist cake is my princesses' *favorite*. They love it so much it has become our official cake for birthdays . . . and just about any other occasion!

For dessert lovers with a food intolerance:
Replace the butter with 7 ounces (200 grams) unsweetened applesauce and the flour with cornstarch.

Who's Who of Princesses
(and Princes!)

Aladdin

Aladdin meets a powerful sorcerer named Jafar who asks him to enter a mysterious cave to find a lamp. But Aladdin is suspicious and refuses to give Jafar the lamp unless he helps him escape the Cave of Wonders. Furious, the sorcerer traps Aladdin in the cave. In the darkness, Aladdin rubs the lamp and discovers that inside it is a genie who can grant him his most extravagant wishes thanks to his extraordinary powers. But Jafar wants to retrieve the lamp and will stop at nothing to use the genie's powers for himself.

Anne of Austria and the Three Musketeers

Anne of Austria was a Spanish princess who went to France to marry the future French king. Lively and mischievous, she enjoyed running up and down the stairs at the Palace of the Louvre (now a world-renowned art museum) and sliding across the parquet floor with her best friend. In Alexandre Dumas's story *The Three Musketeers*, she gives two of her jewels to the Duke of Buckingham as a souvenir of their friendship. But as soon as her enemies learn what she has done, they do everything in their power to ruin her. Anne of Austria cannot go to England herself and asks the faithful D'Artagnan and the courageous musketeers Athos, Porthos, and Aramis to retrieve her diamond studs no matter what adventures they encounter . . .

Sisi

Elisabeth of Wittelsbach was not supposed to become Empress of Austria, but sometimes destiny has other plans. Sisi ascended to the throne beside Franz Joseph and went to live in the Hofburg and Schönbrunn palaces. Having grown up near lakes and forests in Bavaria, she was very bored in Vienna in spite of all the balls and horseback riding, and her obligations as a ruler often weighed heavily on her. This is why she channeled most of her energy into athletics and traveling around Europe.

Snow White

Written by the Brothers Grimm, the story of Snow White recounts the adventures of a young princess with "skin as white as snow, lips as red as blood, and hair as black as ebony." The evil queen, jealous of Snow White's beauty, banishes her to a faraway forest and plots to have her killed. But the Seven Dwarfs teach Snow White that the forest and its animals are not dangerous once you get to know them. Snow White lives happily in her little cottage in the forest—until the day the queen learns that the princess is still alive . . .

Cinderella

Once upon a time, there was a little girl whose parents died of illnesses that might have been prevented by the vaccines we have now. After his wife's death, Cinderella's father remarries a woman who already has two daughters to make sure his daughter won't be alone. But when he dies, the stepmother favors her own children and makes Cinderella a servant in her own house. Fortunately, she is not discouraged and waits patiently for things to fall into place. On the night of a ball, she sees a strange little lady with a magic wand appear: her fairy godmother.

Beauty and the Beast

Transformed by an enchantress into a beastly creature to punish him for his selfishness, a prince shuts himself inside his enchanted castle until the day a poor inventor appears at his door in need of a place to stay. In the morning, the man picks a rose for his daughter, Belle. The Beast is furious and demands that Belle come live at the castle as punishment for her father's theft. Over the course of their time together—in a strange castle where the servants are invisible, torches are held by arms coming out of the walls, and dishes appear and disappear by themselves—Beauty and the Beast learn to get to know and love each other, breaking the spell.

The Little Mermaid

This Hans Christian Andersen story is about a mermaid princess who dreams of discovering the human world after saving a sailor from a terrible storm. In fact, this sailor is actually a prince who wants nothing more than to find the mermaid who saved his life. Determined to meet him, the little mermaid goes to see the sea witch and agrees to exchange her beautiful voice for a pair of legs. Beautiful but unable to speak, the little mermaid must overcome her disability and use her intelligence to make the prince understand who she really is.

The Princess and the Frog

There are two versions of this story, so take your pick: the Russian folktale or the famous Brothers Grimm adaptation. Either way, the prince or princess is transformed into a frog and must be loved for who he or she really is in order to break the spell and become human again. Walt Disney Studios created a brilliant adaptation of this story set in Louisiana in the Roaring Twenties: boisterous music, adventure, twists, and lovable characters: an absolute delight!

The Princess and the Pea

In Hans Christian Andersen's story, a prince wants to choose his own bride instead of marrying one of the princesses his parents are always introducing him to. The night of a storm, a young woman soaked to the skin arrives at the castle and asks for a place to stay. She claims to be a princess. The queen prepares a bed for her made of 20 mattresses and 20 quilts and places a pea at the very bottom. The next day, the queen asks the young woman if she slept well, and she replies that something very hard in the bed kept her from sleeping. The prince is charmed by her honesty, they fall in love, and shortly after the two are married and the pea is placed in the Royal Treasury.

The Snow Queen

There are several versions of this Hans Christian Andersen tale. One of them features a princess and her sister, who happens to be able to control ice and snow. In the traditional version, the Snow Queen takes off in her sleigh and kidnaps a young boy named Kai to bring him back to her ice palace. She freezes his heart to make him forget all about his family and his friend Gerda so he will stay with her forever. Gerda sets out to find Kai and narrowly escapes a witch before finding her friend imprisoned at the palace. When the Snow Queen is away from the palace, Gerda sneaks in and rescues her friend by melting the ice that has frozen his heart and mind.

Leia Organa

Princess Leia Organa is one of the heroines of *Star Wars*. She travels the galaxy to help the Rebels fight against Emperor Palpatine and the terrible Darth Vader. She is highly intelligent, stubborn, and tough, and she is a leader who is listened to and respected. Over the course of her adventures with the Rebellion, Han Solo, and Chewbacca, she discovers Jedi powers and a secret brother, Luke Skywalker.

The Blue Bird

A widowed and very wealthy king leaves his daughter, Princess Florine, in the clutches of his scheming new wife. This new queen wants Prince Charming to choose her own daughter Truitonne as his bride, but he falls in love with Florine. As a result of treachery, traps, and the schemes of enchanters and a fairy godmother, the prince is transformed into a blue bird and Florine finds herself imprisoned in the highest room of the castle's tallest tower . . .

This tale by Madame d'Aulnoy holds a special place in my heart: it is the first one I was able to read by myself!

Merida (Brave)

Merida loves archery and riding with her hair blowing in the wind, but hates obeying the tedious rules imposed by her mother, the queen. After a terrible fight, Merida runs away to the forest. She meets an old woman who offers her a magic cake that can change her destiny. Merida accepts it and gives some to her mother, but as soon as her mother tastes it she is transformed into a bear and must leave the castle before she is hunted and killed. To break the curse and reconcile with each other, mother and daughter will have to learn how to communicate and love one another.

The Princess Bride

Duels, escapes, great love, and miracles—all of this awaits you if you choose to open (or watch) *The Princess Bride*. Westley loves Buttercup. A lowly farmhand, he leaves to make his fortune so he can marry his beloved, but when he does not return everyone assumes he is dead. Overcome with grief, Buttercup closes her heart and swears to never love again. A few years later, Buttercup has become the most beautiful woman in the world and is preparing to marry Prince Humperdinck even though she feels nothing for him. At the same time, four men appear: a cunning Sicilian named Vizzini with plans to kidnap and kill the princess, a Spanish fencing master named Inigo whose heart and sword are searching for the man who killed his father, Fezzik, a giant who is powerful as he is timid, and the man in black, a mysterious and formidable character out for revenge . . .

Shrek

There was once a green ogre named Shrek who lived peacefully in his swamp in the land of fairy tales until the day his quiet marsh became a refuge for fairy tale creatures from our favorite stories (*The Three Little Pigs, Pinocchio, The Gingerbread Man*) who had been exiled from their homes. With the help of Donkey, Shrek goes looking for Princess Fiona, who is being held prisoner in the highest room of the tallest tower of the tallest castle. He unexpectedly falls in love with the princess, but it's not easy to become a prince when you're an ogre.

Adapted from a series of four animated films and filled with incisive humor and unforgettable characters—Puss in Boots, Donkey, and the tenderhearted Dragon—this children's story written by William Steig is now a favorite of "big" kids, too.

Swan Lake

Composed by Pyotr Ilyich Tchaikovsky, *Swan Lake* is a ballet that tells the story of Prince Siegfried and Princess Odette. One beautiful evening, Siegfried spots a beautiful white swan next to a lake who transforms into a magnificent young woman. This is Princess Odette, who was taken from her parents by an evil sorcerer and is now the victim of a powerful spell. She must live as a swan during the day and can only become a princess again when night falls. Siegfried and Odette want to break the spell, but the sorcerer also has a daughter and wants her to marry the prince. So he transforms her into a black swan . . .

Donkey Skin

One day the king's beloved wife dies and makes him promise that he will only marry a woman whose beauty is equal to or greater than her own (the queen was wise, and thought this would protect her dear daughter from falling into the hands of a cruel stepmother).

Years pass and the king keeps his promise. The little princess grows up and becomes more and more beautiful, even lovelier than her mother. One day, the king decides she is the woman he must marry. To escape this union, the princess's fairy godmother advises her to ask her father for things he cannot give her as a way to delay the marriage. When this does not dissuade him, the princess flees to the forest and pretends to be a humble peasant dressed in a donkey's skin . . .

Princess Mononoke

Princess Mononoke or *The Princess of Vengeful Spirits* is a 1997 animated film that has become a cult classic. It tells the story of Ashitaka, Prince of the Emishi, and San, otherwise known as Princess Mononoke, who was raised by the Wolf Goddess Moro. After killing the Boar God, Ashitaka is cursed. To break the curse he must appease Nature's anger. On his journey he arrives in Irontown and finds himself in the midst of a battle between the village's inhabitants and the Forest Spirits. Mononoke and Ashitaka join forces to reconcile the humans and Spirits so they will stop fighting and Nature can find balance once again.

Queen Victoria

As a young girl, Victoria is kept away from the world. She does not go to school and instead has private tutors who come to the castle to teach her the rules of protocol and foreign languages (she speaks English, German, French, Italian, Latin, and Greek). Because she never sees other children, she sometimes gets bored and plays with her dolls or her dog Dash, who is her best friend. Alexandrina Victoria was not born to be queen, and yet she would become one of the most famous rulers of all time and reign over the United Kingdom, Ireland, and far-off countries like India, Australia, and Canada.

Rapunzel

In a story made famous by the Brothers Grimm, a little princess is taken from her parents and held prisoner in a tall tower. The tower has no door and no staircase, and the only way to reach the top is to climb up with the help of Rapunzel's long braid. In the Walt Disney Studios version, Rapunzel uses her hair for acrobatic feats and to heal injuries. She also draws, stargazes, and is rather handy with a frying pan, which she uses to knock out unwanted guests.

Robin Hood

Ah, Robin Hood! The unforgettable hero of Sherwood Forest! Alongside his companions—Little John, Friar Tuck, and the others—he fights relentlessly against the exploitation committed by the Sheriff of Nottingham and Prince John while King Richard the Lionheart is away. An eternal defender of the oppressed who steals from the rich to give to the poor, he becomes a legend for his extraordinary skills with a bow and arrow, his craftiness and audacity, and for his loyalty and love for the delightful Maid Marian. The adventures of Robin Hood have been immortalized in many films and cartoons, but the version with Errol Flynn is one of my favorites!

A Little Princess (Princess Sara)

After living for many years with her father in India, Sara is sent to a boarding school in England. Impressed by her wealth, the director, Miss Minchin, gives her special treatment and makes her the star of the school. But when her father dies, Sara's life is ruined and she is forced to become a servant at the boarding school. One day a mysterious gentleman from India, Mr. Carrisford, moves into the house next door and Sara becomes friends with Ram Dass, his Indian valet. Dass talks to Mr. Carrisford about this strange little servant girl who speaks several languages and knows all about Indian traditions. Mr. Carrisford turns out to be a friend of Sara's father as well as the little girl's legal guardian . . .

She-Ra and the Princesses of Power

Adora is a fearsome soldier in the Horde army. The Horde is commanded by Hordak and rules over the Kingdom of Etheria with an iron fist. After receiving orders to crush the Great Rebellion, Adora enters the Whispering Woods and discovers a magic sword that transforms her into She-Ra. Adora decides to become She-Ra, the princess-heroine of the rebellion, and fulfill her mission to free Etheria. Helped by Bow, Glimmer, and other rebels who all have different powers, she dedicates her life to battling Hordak.

Simba the Lion King

In the heart of the African savanna, a lion cub unlike any other is born: his name is Simba, son of Mufasa and Sarabi. The little prince is quite unruly, and after being manipulated by his uncle Scar he causes a catastrophe that leads to his father's death and his uncle's ascension to the throne. Horrified by what he has done, Simba runs away and meets Timon and Pumbaa, a meerkat and warthog who become his best friends and help him on his journey to adulthood. Now grown up, Simba crosses paths with Nala, his childhood friend. She tells him that the lion kingdom is withering under Scar's paw. Simba has to make a choice: continue to live in hiding or face his uncle and his fears.

Thor

In Scandinavian mythology, Thor is the god of thunder and son of Odin, King of the Gods. Agile but unpredictable, Thor controls the rain and storms and creates lightning with his famous hammer, travelling between worlds to fight the giants, his people's greatest enemies. In film versions, Thor is sent to Earth by Odin, who is fed up with his son's behavior and believes that living without his powers in the company of humans will make Thor less arrogant. But Odin hadn't counted on the plans of cosmic villains to overthrow Asgard and Earth. Thor will have to wise up and find allies if he wants to save them.

Versailles and Trianon

The Palace of Versailles is one of the most beautiful palaces in France, if not the world! The setting for some of the most important moments in French history, this palace was constructed primarily during the reign of King Louis XIV, who was known as the Sun King, and many generations of children grew up there. It is breathtakingly beautiful with magnificent architecture, fountains, and beautifully designed gardens.

The Trianon, located on the edge of the palace grounds, is more discreet: it was the perfect place for the king and queen and their family. They could choose who they wanted to invite and spend time with friends far away from the worries of the kingdom, having fun and truly being themselves.

Desserts to Share

The Princess Bride
"As You Wish" Crumble

Buttercup and Westley lived together on her parents' farm where she prepared delicious desserts with whatever fruits were in season.
Whenever Buttercup asked what kind of fruit Westley wanted in his crumble, he gave the same answer every time: "As you wish."

SERVES 1 PRINCESS, 1 HORRIBLE PIRATE, 1 VENGEFUL SPANIARD, 1 RHYMING GIANT, 1 SIX-FINGERED COUNT, AND 1 KINDHEARTED WITCH

Preparation: 15 minutes

Cooking: 30 minutes

18 ounces (500 grams) pears

18 ounces (500 grams) quinces

7 ounces (200 grams) flour

3½ ounces (100 grams) granulated sugar

3½ ounces (100 grams) butter, cut into small pieces + a little for the baking dish

Preheat the oven to 350°F (180°C, th.6) while the Dread Pirate Roberts makes his way toward the coast of Florin.

Wash the fruit, remove the cores and seeds, then ask Inigo Montoya to cut the fruit into small pieces and transfer them to a buttered baking dish.

Use your fingertips to combine the flour, sugar, and pieces of butter in a bowl until the mixture crumbles between your fingers like sand from the Fire Swamp (or a rock in Fezzik's hand).

Spread your crumble mixture over the fruit and bake for approximately 30 minutes (this is a less dangerous option than waiting for a flame spurt in the swamp).

When the crumble is as golden as Buttercup's hair, enjoy it in good company, perhaps somewhere atop the Cliffs of Insanity.

For dessert lovers with a food intolerance:
Replace the flour with cornstarch.

Donkey Skin
Princely Pastry

When Donkey Skin makes this dessert for the prince, she slips her ring inside. Enchanted by the delicious pastry, the prince asks all of the young girls in the kingdom to try on the ring so he can meet the one who charmed him.

SERVES 6

Preparation: 15 minutes

Cooking: 40 minutes

3½ ounces (100 grams) granulated sugar

2 eggs

1 vanilla bean

1 teaspoon cornstarch

1¾ ounces (50 grams) softened butter

3⅓ fluid ounces (10 cl) milk + a little for decoration

4½ ounces (125 grams) almond flour (or walnut/hazelnut flour)

2 sheets puff-pastry dough (100% butter)

1 gold or silver ring (not plastic!)

Prepare the filling in a bowl: stir together the sugar and eggs.

Cut the vanilla bean in half lengthwise and use the back of a knife to scrape out the seeds. Add the vanilla bean seeds, cornstarch, softened butter, and milk to the bowl and stir until combined. Pour in the almond flour and mix.

Roll out the puff pastry sheets into 2 circles around 12 inches (30 cm) in diameter. Place one circle on a sheet of parchment paper and cover with the almond filling, leaving a ½-inch (1 cm) border around the edge.

Hide the ring in the filling and place the second pastry circle on top. Gently press down the edges of the pastry to make sure the two sheets stick together. And now without further ado, preheat the oven to 350°F (180°C, th. 6).

Use a butter knife to draw a design on top of your pastry. Don't press too hard or you will poke a hole in it. Brush with a little milk and bake for 40 minutes.

Serve hot, warm, or cold—however you like!

She-Ra
Rainbow Diplomates

Diplomacy is definitely a requirement when you're fighting the Horde to save the Kingdom of Etheria. Whether you're a warrior with a talent for teleportation, a commander of ice and plants, or a mermaid, whether you're good with your hands, courageous, or shy, consider yourself welcome among the Princesses of Power (and their prince friends!) with this recipe paying tribute to the colors of She-Ra and Swift Wind, her winged unicorn.

SERVES 8 PRINCES AND PRINCESSES

Preparation: 20 minutes

9 ounces (250 grams) pound cake

14 ounces (400 grams) apricots and peaches (fresh or canned in juice)

10½ ounces (300 grams) blueberry or raspberry jelly

21 ounces (600 grams) vanilla pudding

10½ ounces (300 grams) whipped cream

1 ounce (25 grams) slivered almonds

Using your magic sword, slice the cake into slices ¼-inch (½ cm) thick. Divide the slices into three groups.

Place the first group of cake slices in the bottom of a large clear bowl (or a trifle dish, if you have one, or in several glasses).

Drain the fruit and set aside the juice. Cut into small pieces.

Top the first layer of cake slices with half the fruit and half of the jelly. Then pour half of the vanilla pudding on top. Repeat to create another layer.

Finish with the last group of cake slices and top with whipped cream and slivered almonds.

Refrigerate for a few minutes to give yourself time to transform, then enjoy with friends!

Queen Victoria
Sponge Cake

Before becoming one of the most famous queens of all time, little Victoria was an intelligent and mischievous girl who loved treats. This cake was created in her honor.

SERVES 8 OF THE QUEEN'S SUBJECTS

Preparation: 10 minutes

Resting: 15 minutes

Cooking: 40 minutes

3½ ounces (100 grams) softened butter

3½ ounces (100 grams) granulated sugar

2 eggs

3½ ounces (100 grams) flour

1 teaspoon (5½ grams) baking powder

2½ ounces (75 grams) raspberry compote, unsweetened

2 single-serving containers of vanilla pudding (lactose-free if necessary)

Powdered sugar for decoration

In a beautiful flowered bowl, mix the butter and sugar together. Add the eggs one at a time and stir carefully. Next sift the flour and baking powder into the bowl and stir.

Pour the batter into two round molds and bake for 20 to 25 minutes at 400°F (200°C, th. 6-7) until each sponge is golden and springs back when pressed.

Let cool for about 15 minutes, which is just enough time to set up a table in the middle of the rose garden.

Spread the raspberry compote over one cake, top with the vanilla pudding, and place the second cake on top, pressing down very gently to hold everything together.

Dust with powdered sugar and serve in the garden . . . hopefully you won't have to come running back in when it starts raining!

For dessert lovers with a food intolerance:
Replace the flour with cornstarch and the butter with unsweetened applesauce.

Robin Hood, Prince of Thieves

Sherwood Blackberry Tart

Just because you live in the middle of the forest and spend your time escaping from the Sheriff of Nottingham doesn't mean you can't enjoy a sweet treat now and then. Try this blackberry tart created by Friar Tuck himself—I know you're going to love it!

SERVES 8 JOYFUL COMPANIONS

Preparation: 15 minutes

Cooking: 35 minutes

1 premade piecrust

2½ ounces (70 grams) hazelnuts

2 egg whites

Pinch of salt

1¾ ounces (50 grams) granulated sugar

9 ounces (250 grams) blackberry jelly

Preheat the oven to 350°F (180°C, th.6).

Press the piecrust into a tart pan and use the tip of an arrow to poke holes in it. This will ensure that it stays flat during baking and won't puff up like the Sheriff of Nottingham's belly.

Bake the crust for 20 minutes while you grab your bow, your quiver, and your best pair of green tights!

Crush the hazelnuts into little pieces.

In a (clean) bowl or helmet (also clean), beat the egg whites with the salt into stiff peaks, then add the sugar carefully to keep the whites from deflating.

Remove the tart pan from the oven—careful, it will be hot.

Spread the jelly over the piecrust, cover with the meringue you just made, and sprinkle with hazelnuts. Bake for 15 minutes until the top turns the golden brown of autumn leaves.

This is perfect for a banquet in the forest or a snack before the greatest archery tournament in all of England.

Princess Mononoke
Tea-Tofu Cheesecake

While Lady Eboshi and the emperor's forces are trying to destroy the Forest Spirits, San (Princess Mononoke) and Prince Ashitaka take hiding on the Deer God's island to recover from their injuries before returning to battle to save the forest.

SERVES 4 FOREST SPIRITS

Preparation: 15 minutes

Steeping: 15 minutes

Cooking: 1 hour

Refrigeration: 2 hours

For the tart base

7 ounces (200 grams) butter cookies or ladyfingers

5 tablespoons almond puree

3 tablespoons nondairy milk (almond, oat, etc.)

For the filling

10½ ounces (300 grams) rice milk

1 green tea bag

14 ounces (400 grams) firm silken tofu

2 eggs

5 ounces (140 grams) brown sugar

1 tablespoon (14 grams) vanilla sugar

1¾ ounces (50 grams) cornstarch

Preheat the oven to 350°F (180°C, th.6).

Heat the milk in a saucepan over low heat, then place the tea bag in the milk and steep for around 15 minutes. Remove the tea bag.

Crush the cookies in a food processor until they form a powder. In a large bowl, mix this powder with the almond puree and the nondairy milk to form a soft dough you can roll into a ball.

Line a tart pan with parchment paper and press the dough into the pan. Bake for 15 minutes.

Stir together the tofu, eggs, green tea–infused milk, sugars, and cornstarch.

Remove the tart base from the oven and add the filling. Bake for 45 minutes.

Let cool and refrigerate for at least 2 hours.

Desserts
Just for You

Rapunzel
Sweet Omelette

How are you supposed to spend the day if you're locked in a tower? Looking at stars and birds? Maybe, instead, you become a professional climber and pay a visit to the garden next door . . . you were named after one of the flowers growing in it!

SERVES 1 PRINCESS, 1 ROBBER-PRINCE, AND 2 FRIENDS

Preparation: 10 minutes

Cooking: 25 minutes

18 ounces (500 grams) rhubarb

1 tablespoon water

6 eggs

1 tablespoon crème fraîche

4 tablespoons vanilla sugar

1½ ounces (40 grams) butter

As soon as the witch's back is turned, let down your hair and go pick some of the rhubarb growing in the old garden.

Rinse the rhubarb and peel if needed to remove any sections that are too fibrous (Yuck! Even a chameleon wouldn't want that).

Next cut the rhubarb into small pieces and add to a saucepan with 1 tablespoon of water. Cook for 20 minutes over a flame as gentle and soft as your hair.

Crack the eggs into a bowl and beat with the crème fraîche and sugar.

Add the rhubarb compote to the bowl. Stir until combined.

Melt the butter over low heat in your favorite pan, pour in the omelette mixture, and cook for 5 minutes over high heat until it's the same beautiful golden color as your hair.

Slide the omelette onto a plate and place under the broiler to caramelize while you help your friends climb up the tower.

For dessert lovers with a food intolerance:
Replace the crème fraîche with nondairy cream.

Thor Entremets

This take on rice pudding is one of the most beloved desserts in the land of Thor.

SERVES 6 ASGARDIAN WARRIORS

Preparation: 20 minutes

Resting: 10 minutes

Cooking: 40 minutes

18 ounces (500 grams) short-grain rice

½ vanilla bean

34 fluid ounces (1 liter) milk

3½ ounces (100 grams) almonds

3½ ounces (100 grams) honey

4½ ounces (125 grams) whipped cream

9 ounces (250 grams) pitted cherries

Rinse the rice and pour into a pot of water. Summon lightning to make it boil for 5 minutes.

Slice open the vanilla bean and scrape out the seeds. Add the seeds to the milk.

Drain the rice and return it to the pot along with the milk. Simmer over low heat for 35 minutes, uncovered.

Break the almonds into large pieces. You can use a hammer, a knife, or the bottom of a pot.

When the rice is tender, add the honey, stir, and let cool in the frozen North or in the refrigerator.

Top with whipped cream, cherries, and almonds, and wherever you are, call Heimdall and ask him to open the doors to the Kingdom of Odin so you can enjoy your dessert in good company.

For dessert lovers with a food intolerance:
Replace the milk with nondairy milk and the whipped cream with almond milk whipped cream.

Beauty and the Beast
Rose Mousseline Cream

When Belle comes to live at the castle, she and the Beast aren't exactly on the best of terms yet.
The servants prepare an enormous feast to lighten the mood.

SERVES 4

Preparation: 15 minutes

Refrigeration: 2 hours

2 gelatin sheets

4 tablespoons rose water

10½ ounces (300 grams) fresh raspberries (or frozen raspberries, thawed and drained)

1 tablespoon honey

18 ounces (500 grams) plain yogurt

2 egg whites

Pinch of salt

2 tablespoon powdered sugar

A few edible rose petals

Start by softening the gelatin sheets in a large bowl of cold water for 5 minutes.

While you wait, ask one of your kind servants to heat the rose water in a small saucepan over low heat.

When the gelatin is as wobbly as your knees when you're exploring the castle, add it to the rose water.

In a large bowl, stir together the raspberries, honey, and yogurt. Add the rose water and gelatin.

In a separate bowl, beat the egg whites with the salt into stiff peaks. The whites are ready when they are as frothy and fluffy as newly fallen snow—and if they don't fall on your head when you turn the bowl upside down. Sprinkle the powdered sugar over the egg whites and incorporate it gently to keep them from deflating.

Add the beaten egg whites to the yogurt-raspberry mixture, spoon into cups, and chill for 2 hours.

Sprinkle with rose petals and serve in the library, at the ball, or in between snowball fights!

For dessert lovers with a food intolerance:
Replace the plain yogurt with nondairy yogurt.

The Princess and the Frog
Bayou Pancakes

Tiana dreams of having her own restaurant . . . In the meantime, her pancakes are already a hit!

SERVES 4 ALLIGATORS (12 PANCAKES)

Preparation: 10 minutes

Cooking: 4 minutes per pancake + 5 minutes under the broiler

18 ounces (500 grams) flour

2 teaspoons (11 grams) baking powder

2 ounces (60 grams) granulated sugar

17 fluid ounces (½ liter) milk

1 vanilla bean

4 bananas

4 teaspoons brown sugar

2 pinches ground cinnamon

Handful of chopped pecans

In a cabin in the middle of the bayou—and also in a bowl—stir together the flour and baking powder. Add the sugar and the milk. Combine using a whisk.

Cut the vanilla bean in half lengthwise—watch your fingers!—and scrape out the seeds with the back of a knife. Add these to the mixture and whisk together in time to the boisterous music of the bayou!

Pour 2 tablespoons of batter into a nonstick pan, flatten to form a small circle, cook for 2 minutes on each side, and set aside somewhere hungry hands can't reach.

If you are in your frog form, wipe off the slime from your hands and feet. If you are in human form, do the same and then peel the bananas before slicing them into rounds.

Place 3 pancakes on each plate followed by the banana slices. Sprinkle with brown sugar and cinnamon, top with the pecans, and set under the broiler for 5 minutes.

For dessert lovers with a food intolerance:
Replace the milk with oat milk and the flour with cornstarch.

The Little Mermaid
Seaweed and Raspberry Shortbread

These little cookies are so old that people have been enjoying them since Hans Christian Andersen's time. This is the perfect version for a mermaid who also wants to live on land.

MAKES 8 COOKIES

Preparation: 15 minutes

Resting: 45 minutes

Cooking: 12 minutes

7 ounces (200 grams) fresh raspberries (or thawed frozen raspberries)

Pinch of agar-agar powder

Drizzle of honey

7 ounces (200 grams) softened butter

10½ ounces (300 grams) flour

4½ ounces (125 grams) powdered sugar

Juice of 1 lemon

Rainbow sprinkles

Rinse the raspberries in fresh water, then blend with an immersion blender, mixer, or blender. If you don't have one, crush the fruit and press the puree through a fine-mesh strainer.

Place a small saucepan over medium heat, pour in the raspberry puree, and when heated add the agar-agar powder. Stir well. Taste and add a little bit of honey, but not too much, because you want the puree to be a little tart. Pour into a bowl and let cool.

Make the cookie dough by combining the butter and flour. Divide into two balls, wrap them in a damp towel, and let rest 30 minutes in the refrigerator.

Preheat the oven to 350°F (180°C, th.6).

Roll out the balls of dough into 10-inch (25 cm) squares. Refrigerate for 15 minutes on a baking tray (or your oven's drip pan) lined with parchment paper. Bake the cookie squares for 12 minutes each at 400°F (200°C, th.6–7) until golden.

Let the ocean breeze cool the squares and cut each one into eight pieces (2^1/$_2$ inches x 5 inches / 6 cm x 12 cm).

Spread the raspberry puree on half of the cookies and top each one with a second cookie.

In a small bowl, dissolve the powdered sugar in the lemon juice. Quickly pour it on top of the cookies as a glaze and top with sprinkles.

Enjoy on the beach while listening to the song of the waves.

For dessert lovers with a food intolerance:
Replace the flour with cornstarch.

Snow White
Baked Apples

We know that Snow White *loves* apples—they were almost her undoing! Here is one of her favorite recipes: it's simple, quick, and delicious. And since it doesn't require very many ingredients, you can even make it in a cottage in the middle of nowhere.

SERVES 1 PRINCESS AND 7 DWARFS

Preparation: 10 minutes

Cooking: 30 minutes

8 apples

8 teaspoons red currant jelly

3½ ounces (100 grams) raisins

2 ounces (60 grams) butter

4 tablespoons granulated sugar

Preheat the oven to 350°F (180°C, th.6) while humming a joyful tune.

Rinse the apples and scoop out the core and seeds. Place them in a baking dish.

Fill each apple with 1 teaspoon of red currant jelly, add the raisins, and top with a little more jelly.

Place a pat of butter on top of each apple and sprinkle with sugar.

Bake for 30 minutes and serve warm while you listen to the birds singing.

For dessert lovers with a food intolerance:
Replace the butter with unsweetened applesauce.

Author's Note:
For this recipe to be a success, you absolutely must whistle while you work.

The Snow Queen
Frosty Popsicles

Whether it's freezing cold or bright and sunny, whether the Snow Queen has frozen the earth or has somehow lost her powers, whatever the season, enjoy these popsicles that come straight from the land of ice . . .

MAKES 6 POPSICLES

Preparation: 10 minutes

Freezing: 3 hours

6 popsicle or lollipop molds or 12 small yogurt containers (empty)

During blueberry season

18 ounces (500 grams) fresh blueberries (not frozen)

14 ounces (400 grams) sweetened condensed milk

When blueberries are not in season

1 bottle Cool Blue Raspberry Gatorade®

1 bottle sugarcane syrup

During blueberry season, rinse the berries and drain them thoroughly, then blend them with the condensed milk in a food processor.

Pour the mixture through a strainer to remove any large pieces.

Pour the blueberry milk into your popsicle molds (or yogurt containers large enough to stick a teaspoon into).

Freeze them with the tips of your fingers or place them in the freezer for at least 3 hours.

When blueberries are not in season, mix 1 part sugarcane syrup with 6 or 7 parts blue raspberry drink.

Pour into the molds and place in the freezer for at least 3 hours, unless of course you have magical powers . . .

For dessert lovers with a food intolerance:
Replace the milk with almond cream and 1¾ ounces (50 grams) powdered sugar.

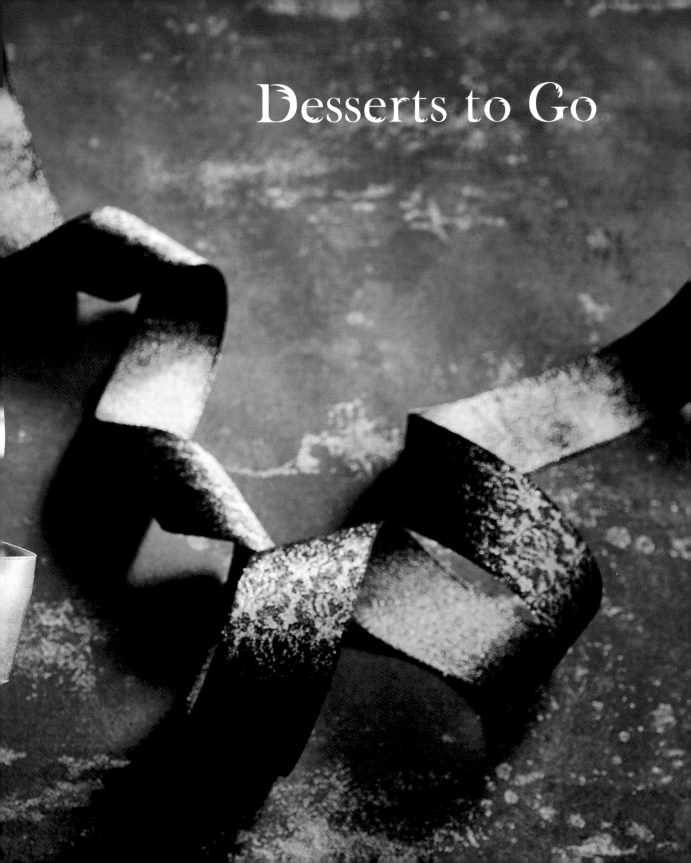

Desserts to Go

Aladdin
Baklava from the Souk

Aladdin grew up in the streets of Agrabah and loves walking through the market. You can find everything there: merchandise from the four corners of the earth, a thousand different spices, delicious pastries, and even princesses who like exploring.

MAKES 30 TREATS

Preparation: 30 minutes

Cooking: 50 minutes

18 ounces (500 grams) pistachios, almonds, and hazelnuts

½ teaspoon ground cinnamon

9 ounces (250 grams) butter

1 package phyllo dough (10-12 sheets)

9 ounces (250 grams) granulated sugar

9 ounces (250 grams) water

Juice of 1 lemon

4½ ounces (125 grams) honey

Preheat the oven to 350°F (180°C, th.6).

Crush the pistachios, almonds, and hazelnuts (in a mixer or blender) and combine with the cinnamon.

Melt the butter for 1 minute in the microwave or 5 minutes in a saucepan over low heat.

Roll out the phyllo dough and cut it to fit the dimensions of your baking pan (mine is 8 x 8 inches / 20 x 20 cm).

Place two phyllo sheets at the bottom of the pan and brush with butter.

Sprinkle with the nut and cinnamon mixture. Repeat and finish with 6 sheets of phyllo dough.

Draw 5 rows and 6 columns on the top of your pastry with a knife, slightly less if your pan is small and slightly more if your pan is large.

Cut along these lines without separating the squares from each other, then bake for 50 minutes until golden brown.

Just before the pastry is finished baking, mix the sugar and water in a saucepan over high heat. When bubbles start to appear, add the lemon juice and honey, lower the heat, and simmer for 20 minutes.

Remove the baklava from the oven, pour the syrup over it—be careful not to burn yourself—and let cool completely before enjoying these treats as you admire the lights of Agrabah reflecting off the Red Sea . . .

Simba
Lion Cub Bites

When you're the prince of the savanna and have to handle everything from wildebeest stampedes to scheming hyenas, sometimes you need a little something nice to lift your spirits . . .

MAKES 12 BITES

Preparation: 15 minutes

Refrigeration: 2 hours

Cooking: 10 minutes

5¼ ounces (150 grams) milk chocolate

3½ ounces (100 grams) butter

9 ounces (250 grams) marshmallows

4½ ounces (130 grams) puffed rice cakes

Ask an elephant or hippopotamus friend to break the chocolate into pieces, then melt it with the butter beneath the merciless rays of the savanna sun. You can also use a saucepan over medium heat.

Cut the marshmallows into quarters and add to the previous mixture.

Carefully crumble the rice cakes into tiny pieces or crush with a rolling pin.

Remove the saucepan from the heat and pour in the pieces of rice cake. Stir to make sure all of the rice cake pieces are coated.

Transfer the mixture to the silicone molds of your choice (animals, half-spheres, or whatever you have at home!) and press down firmly with your paws.

Chill for at least 2 hours and remove from the mold with your claws.

Purr with pleasure as you enjoy these treats with your furry and feathered friends.

Sisi
Austrian Knödel

Ever since her childhood in Bavaria, Sisi always had a passion for horses and long walks in the forest. Here's a recipe for a dessert she might have enjoyed with her family during their summers by the lake.

MAKES 12 KNÖDEL

Preparation: 15 minutes

Refrigeration: 30 minutes

Cooking: 20 minutes

12 apricots

9 ounces (250 grams) fromage blanc

3¾ ounces (110 grams) brown sugar, divided

1 tablespoon (14 grams) vanilla sugar

1¾ ounces (50 grams) softened butter

1 egg

3½ ounces (100 grams) flour

Wash the apricots and remove the pits without separating the halves of the fruits. You can use the handle of a wooden spoon to push out the pits—this does not require any cutting.

Mix the fromage blanc with 2 ounces (60 grams) of brown sugar, the vanilla sugar, the butter, and the egg. Then sift in the flour.

Form a ball of dough, wrap it in a towel, and refrigerate for 30 minutes.

Place 1 teaspoon of brown sugar in each apricot.

Put a large pot of water on to boil.

Roll out the dough to a thickness of ¼ inch (½ cm) using a rolling pin. Cut out pieces large enough to wrap around each apricot, and secure the dough around the fruit.

Place these little dumplings in boiling water using a slotted spoon. Cook for 15 minutes, then carefully drain. When they are completely dry, roll them in the remaining brown sugar and place them under the broiler just long enough for the sugar to caramelize.

Enjoy while gazing upon the beautiful blue Danube . . .

For dessert lovers with a food intolerance:
Replace the flour with cornstarch.

Leja

Rebel Brioches

A traditional breakfast on Alderaan . . .

MAKES 25 MINI BRIOCHES

Preparation: 25 minutes

Resting: 1 hour 30 minutes

Cooking: 5–10 minutes

1¼ ounces (35 grams) fresh yeast

10 fluid ounces (30 cl) milk, divided

4 ounces (120 grams) butter

26 ounces (750 grams) flour

1 tablespoon baking powder (or baking soda)

1 egg

Pinch of salt

3½ ounces (100 grams) granulated sugar

Filling

4 ounces (120 grams) softened butter

1¾ ounces (50 grams) brown sugar

2 tablespoons ground cinnamon

Icing

1 egg

2 tablespoons water

2 tablespoons pearl sugar

Ask your favorite droid to crumble the yeast into pieces and dissolve it in a bowl with 2 tablespoons warm milk. Let rest for 15 minutes.

Melt the butter for 1 minute in the microwave or 5 minutes in a saucepan over low heat.

Sift the flour and baking powder into a large bowl, then add the butter, egg, salt, sugar, and the remaining milk. Knead for 10 minutes.

Cover the dough and let rest for 45 minutes in a warm place away from any airflow (do not leave it near a spaceship engine, for example).

Use the power of the Force to make the filling by combining the butter, sugar, and cinnamon in a bowl. You will eventually have a cream as smooth as a smuggler's smile.

Roll out the dough into a strip as wide as a Wookie's hand (12 inches / 30 cm) and as thick as one of their hairs (3–5 mm). Brush on the cream and roll up the dough to form a long sausage shape. Use your lightsaber to make 25 slices (it's more precise than a phaser).

Let rest for another 45 minutes directly on a baking tray and cover with a damp towel to keep the dough from drying out.

Preheat the oven to 425°F (220°C, th.7–8).

Beat the egg and water in a bowl, brush the brioches, sprinkle with pearl sugar, and bake for 5 to 10 minutes.

For dessert lovers with a food intolerance:
Replace the flour with cornstarch.

Swan Lake
Black and White Swans

Siegfried is a young prince who wants to be free to do what he wants. Odette is a princess who transforms into a white swan as soon as the sun rises, and Odile is a black swan as well as the daughter of a powerful magician. What would you like to be?

MAKES 18 SWANS

Preparation: 20 minutes

Refrigeration: 15 minutes

Cooking: 20 minutes

Vanilla swans

2 ounces (60 grams) granulated sugar

2 ounces (60 grams) softened butter

1 tablespoon milk

3¼ ounces (90 grams) flour

½ teaspoon baking powder

1 ounce (30 grams) instant vanilla pudding mix

Chocolate swans

2 ounces (60 grams) granulated sugar

2 ounces (60 grams) softened butter

1 tablespoon milk

3¼ ounces (90 grams) flour

½ teaspoon baking powder

1 ounce (30 grams) cocoa powder

For the vanilla swans:

In a large bowl, combine the sugar and butter. Add the milk. Sift the flour, baking powder, and pudding mix into the bowl.

Place the dough between 2 large sheets of parchment paper and roll it out to a thickness of about ¼ inch (½ cm). Refrigerate for 15 minutes while you prepare the dough for the chocolate swans.

For the chocolate swans:

Repeat the same steps you used to make the vanilla swans, but replace the pudding mix with cocoa powder.

Preheat the oven to 400°F (200°C, th.6–7).

Remove the top sheet of parchment paper and cut out the swans with a cookie cutter or stencil (see note).

Place the swans on a baking tray lined with parchment paper and bake for around 20 minutes.

Let the cookies cool and serve at sunset with the marvelous music of Tchaikovsky in the background.

Tip: You can make your own swan-shaped cookie cutter by drawing (or tracing!) on a thin piece of cardboard and cutting it out to use as an outline.

For dessert lovers with a food intolerance:
Replace the flour with cornstarch and the milk with nondairy milk.

The Princess and the Pea

Pink Peas

The best way to know whether you're dealing with a real prince or princess is to make them taste these little peas . . . Only true royalty can detect which treats are the tastiest.

MAKES 15–20 PINK PEAS

Preparation: 20 minutes

Resting: 2 hours

7 ounces (200 grams) pink ladyfinger cookies (biscuits roses de Reims)

3½ ounces (100 grams) almond flour

1¾ ounces (50 grams) honey

2–3 tablespoons milk

Place the cookies in a food processor and reduce to a powder as fine as the drizzle that has been falling since early this morning.

Measure out 3½ ounces (100 grams) of cookie powder and set aside the rest for the end of the recipe. In a large bowl, combine the remaining 3½ ounces (100 grams) cookie powder with the almond flour, then add the honey and the milk, little by little.

Knead well to combine the ingredients, then form a ball of dough that is not sticky but not falling apart, either. If the dough is too sticky, add a little almond flour. If it is crumbly, add a tiny bit of milk.

Form 1-inch balls of dough, roll them in the remaining cookie powder, and refrigerate for 2 hours.

Now all you have to do is place these peas under the mattress of a princess (or prince!) to be sure they are exactly who they say they are . . . well, if there are any peas left after snacktime, that is!

Princess Sara
Magic Muffins

One night, exhausted after a day of hard work, Sara goes up to her room in the attic. She thinks she must be dreaming when she sees a warm muffin, soft quilts, a nightgown, and new slippers waiting for her. The same thing happens the next day—is it magic?

MAKES 12 MUFFINS

Preparation: 15 minutes

Cooking: 45 minutes

2¾ ounces (80 grams) candied fruit (cherries, oranges, lemons, angelica)

3½ ounces (100 grams) flour + a little for the candied fruit

1 teaspoon (5½ grams) baking powder

3¾ ounces (110 grams) brown sugar

3¾ ounces (110 grams) softened butter

2 eggs

2¾ ounces (80 grams) raisins

2¾ ounces (80 grams) nuts (walnuts, hazelnuts, almonds . . .)

Preheat the oven to 350°F (180°C, th.6).

Cut the candied fruit into small cubes, then dust them with a little flour to keep them from sticking together.

Sift the flour and baking powder into a large bowl, add the sugar and softened butter, then the eggs one at a time. Stir until you have a nice dough without any lumps. Add the candied fruit, raisins, and nuts.

Mix well and transfer the batter to a muffin tin, filling each muffin cup about two-thirds full to allow the muffins to puff up.

Bake for around 45 minutes. You will know the muffins are done when the blade of a knife inserted in the center comes out clean.

Serve in the attic or in a palace, but make sure you're surrounded by your best friends!

For dessert lovers with a food intolerance:
Replace the butter with unsweetened applesauce and the flour with cornstarch.

Hall of Mirrors
Croissants

The Hall of Mirrors at Versailles is truly a marvel! Imagine how much fun it must have been to have slip-and-slide competitions there!

MAKES ROUGHLY 12 CROISSANTS

Preparation: 30 minutes

Resting: 1 hour 45 minutes

Cooking: 20 minutes

1 cube fresh yeast (1½ ounces)

8½ fluid ounces (25 cl) warm milk + a little for decoration

18 ounces (500 grams) flour

2 ounces (60 grams) powdered sugar

Pinch of salt

7 ounces (200 grams) butter

Crumble the yeast into a bowl and dissolve in the warm milk. Cover and let rest in a warm place for 15 minutes.

Sift the flour into a large bowl and mix in the sugar, salt, and yeast to form your dough. Roll it out on a flat surface.

Cut the butter into thin slices and sprinkle them over the dough. Fold the dough in quarters and refrigerate for 15 minutes. Remove the dough from the refrigerator, roll it out again, fold it in quarters again, and refrigerate for 15 minutes. Then roll it out one last time and cut out 12 triangles. Roll up each triangle into a crescent shape, starting from the wide end.

Line a baking tray with parchment paper. Place the croissants on the tray and let them rise for 1 hour at room temperature.

Preheat the oven to 350°F (180°C, th.6).

Brush the croissants with milk and bake for 20 minutes.

Take a few croissants and lie down on the floor in the Hall of Mirrors to appreciate the paintings on the ceiling before the courtiers arrive . . .

For dessert lovers with a food intolerance:
Replace the flour with cornstarch, the milk with nondairy milk, and the sugar with honey.

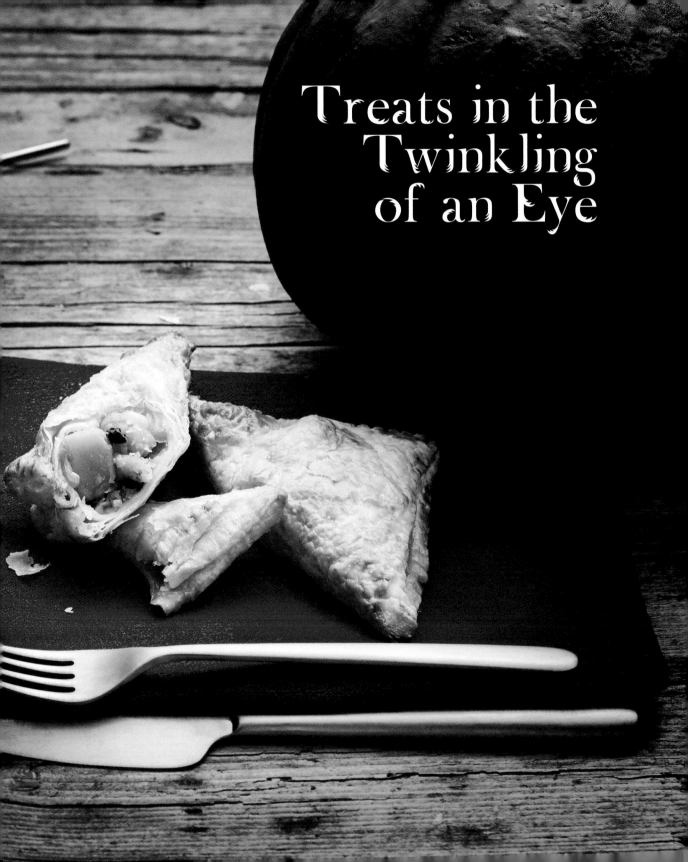

Treats in the
Twinkling
of an Eye

Anne of Austria
Three Musketeers Hot Chocolate

Anne of Austria was made famous by the story of *The Three Musketeers*: it is on her behalf that D'Artagnan, Athos, Porthos, and Aramis risk the danger of confronting the terrible Cardinal Richelieu. To me, this princess is also very important because she introduced chocolate to my country, France.

SERVES 4 MUSKETEERS

Preparation and cooking:
15 minutes

2½ ounces (75 grams) dark chocolate bar

13½ fluid ounces (40 cl) milk

1 orange

Drizzle of honey

Whipped cream

Break the chocolate into pieces and melt them with the milk in a saucepan over low heat while Princess Anne slides down the castle halls.

Cut the orange in half with a sharp knife and juice it. Use a small strainer to remove the seeds (lace sleeves are not a good idea).

When the chocolate is melted, stir it well, then add the orange juice and honey.

Taste and then pour into mugs. Top with a little cream as white as the feather in your hat and hurry to face the cardinal's guards!

For dessert lovers with a food intolerance:
Replace the milk with almond or oat milk and do not add whipped cream.

Shrek
Swamp Mousse Cake

When you marry a princess, you become a prince—Shrek the ogre should know. When he is forced to travel to the Kingdom of Far Far Away, Shrek gets the blues. Here's a green and mossy mug cake to help remind him of his beloved swamp.

SERVES 1

Preparation: 5 minutes

Cooking: 2 minutes

¾ ounce (20 grams) butter

1 tablespoon honey

1 tablespoon pistachio paste

1 egg

1½ ounces (40 grams) flour

½ teaspoon baking powder

Ask Donkey to melt the butter in a bowl for 30 seconds in the microwave—that will keep him busy.

Add the honey and pistachio paste, then the egg.

Sift the flour and baking powder into a large bowl and add to the previous mixture. Stir until there are no lumps and the whole mixture has the same greenish color as the wonderful swamp mud that smells so good.

Transfer to a mug and microwave on high for 1 minute, 30 seconds (or just ask Dragon to blow on the mug).

Enjoy immediately, dreaming of the peaceful solitude of your beautiful mossy swamp.

For dessert lovers with a food intolerance:
Replace the butter with unsweetened applesauce and the flour with cornstarch.

Merida
Highland Blend

Merida wants to be a princess but doesn't want to give up the things she loves: archery, riding horses, and exploring the Scottish hills. That shouldn't be too much to ask!

SERVES 6

Preparation: 15 minutes

Cooking: 5 minutes

18 ounces (500 grams) summer berries (raspberries, wild strawberries, gooseberries . . .)

6 tablespoons rolled oats

9 ounces (250 grams) whipped cream

When the highlands are hiding in the mist and the heather is still wet with dew, run through the moors and look for berries to make your dessert (don't use your bow and arrow to pick them or you'll get juice everywhere).

Back at the castle, after rescuing your shoes from the peat bog, spread out the oats on a baking tray lined with parchment paper and toast for 5 minutes under the broiler. Stay nearby, because they burn quickly! Let cool for 10 minutes.

Rinse the fruit in fresh water from a waterfall and dry carefully.

In a pretty cup, alternate layers of fruit, cream, and a pinch of toasted oats. Finish the top layer with oats.

Place the cups in a basket, brave the thistles surrounding the castle, and enjoy your snack from atop Hadrian's Wall while you watch red deer and bears returning to the forest . . .

For dessert lovers with a food intolerance:
Replace the whipped cream with whipped almond cream.

Cinderella
Pumpkin Turnovers

Is Cinderella nothing but a lowly servant in her own home? Absolutely not! She is an excellent dressmaker and can even communicate with animals!

SERVES 1 FAIRY, 1 PRINCE, 1 PRINCESS, 2 MICE, AND 1 HORSE

Preparation: 15 minutes

Cooking: 15-20 minutes

Flour for your work surface

18 ounces (500 grams) puff pastry dough

18 ounces (500 grams) cooked pumpkin (or squash)

6 teaspoons raisins

6 teaspoons honey

A little milk

When Lucifer the cat has finished napping on the table, wash it off and sprinkle a little flour over it. Roll out your puff pastry with a rolling pin to form a large rectangle roughly 16 x 24 inches (40 x 60 cm) in size. Cut it into 6 squares.

Preheat the oven to 350°F (180°C, th.6), then ask the mice to take out a large bowl and stir together the pumpkin, raisins, and honey.

Place 2 to 3 tablespoons of this mixture on the lower half of each puff-pastry square, above one of the corners. Make sure to leave a finger's width between the filling and the edge.

Dip your finger in water and wet the edges of your square. Fold down the opposite corner over the filling so your square becomes a triangle.

Press down on the edges with a fork to seal them (or ask your little bird friends to joyfully jump on them).

Repeat this process with the remaining ingredients and place the turnovers on a baking tray lined with parchment paper.

Brush the turnovers with milk and bake for 15 to 20 minutes until they are golden and crispy to your liking.

The Blue Bird
Fruit Salad

At the time *The Blue Bird* was written, the King of France was nicknamed the Sun King and loved fruit. His favorite fruits became very fashionable, and I was inspired by the tastes of this great ruler to create this recipe worthy of a prince.

SERVES 1 PRINCESS, 1 PRINCE, 2 FAIRIES, 1 MAGICIAN, AND 2 VILLAINS

Preparation: 15 minutes

1 bunch of grapes

2 peaches

3 apricots

6 strawberries or 3 figs

2 pears

1 vanilla bean

6 tablespoons honey

Ask Monsieur de La Quintinie, the royal gardener, to harvest the fruit for you. Then rinse it under water from a fountain (Apollo's Basin, for example) and hurry off to the palace kitchens.

Cut the grapes in half and the rest of the fruit into pieces. Don't forget to remove seeds and pits. Divide the fruit into 7 bowls.

Cut the vanilla bean in half lengthwise and scrape out the seeds with the tip of a knife.

Add the vanilla bean seeds to the fruit, top with honey, and gently mix without crushing the fruit.

To enjoy this dessert with the prince, just go to the grove where the blue bird hides and say the magic words:

Bird as blue as cloudless sky,

Hither, hither quickly fly!

For dessert lovers with a food intolerance:
If, like the Sun King, you are allergic to strawberries, do what he did and replace them with figs.

Grand Trianon
Macarons

This recipe is different from the one we're familiar with today, but it is exactly the one that young princes and princesses enjoyed 250 years ago while frolicking in the gardens of Versailles and Trianon.

MAKES 10–12 MACARONS

Preparation: 2 minutes

Cooking: 15 minutes

4 egg whites

9 ounces (250 grams) granulated sugar

9 ounces (250 grams) almond flour

Preheat the oven to 350°F (180°C, th.6).

In a large bowl, beat the egg whites with the sugar and almond flour.

Use a spoon to form small balls of dough and place them on a baking tray lined with parchment paper.

Flatten the balls a little if needed and bake for 15 minutes until the macarons are a blond color but not yet golden brown.

These are ready to nibble on as soon as they are cool enough not to burn your fingers.

Orangerie
Madeleines

Back when little princes and princesses were growing up at Versailles, oranges were very rare. So rare and precious, in fact, that a special place was built just for them: the Orangerie. This building still exists and houses the palace's orange and lemon trees every winter.

MAKES ABOUT 20 MADELEINES

Preparation: 10 minutes

Cooking: 16 minutes

2 eggs

2¾ ounces (80 grams) granulated sugar

2¾ ounces (80 grams) flour

1 teaspoon (5½ grams) baking powder

2¾ ounces (80 grams) softened butter

1 drop sweet orange essential oil (or lemon/mandarin)

Preheat the oven to 350°F (180°C, th.6).

Crack the eggs into a large bowl, then add the sugar and beat until the mixture whitens.

Sift the flour and baking powder and add to the previous mixture.

Melt the butter in a saucepan over low heat and pour gradually into the previous mixture.

Carefully add just 1 drop of the essential oil—the flavor is very powerful.

Stir one last time and pour into your madeleine molds, filling them two-thirds full so they can puff up while baking.

Bake for 10 minutes in the center of the oven, then place the oven rack at the lowest position and bake for 6 more minutes.

Enjoy with your family to the sound of the marvelous burbling of the garden fountains (or anywhere with people you like).

For dessert lovers with a food intolerance:
Replace the flour with cornstarch and the butter with unsweetened applesauce.

Useful Measurements

1 TEASPOON =
→ $^1/_5$ oz (5 g) of salt, sugar, oil, or butter
→ $^1/_5$ fl oz (0.50 cl) of liquid
→ $^1/_5$ oz (5 g) of flour or semolina

1 TABLESPOON =
→ 0.50 oz (15 g) of sugar, flour, oil, or crème fraîche
→ 0.50 fl oz (1.5 cl) of liquid
→ 3 tsp

PINCH OF SALT =
→ $^1/_{16}$ TSP (0.30–0.50 G)

Oven Temperatures

THERMOSTAT	APPROXIMATE TEMPERATURE
1	85°F (30°C) barely lukewarm
2	140°F (60°C) warm
3	195°F (90°C) very low heat
4	250°F (120°C) low heat
5	300°F (150°C) moderate heat
6	350°F (180°C) medium heat
7	410°F (210°C) fairly hot
8	460°F (240°C) hot
9	520°F (270°C) very hot
10	570°F (300°C) high heat

METRIC AND IMPERIAL CONVERSIONS
(These conversions are rounded for convenience)

Ingredient	Cups/Tablespoons/Teaspoons	Ounces	Grams/Milliliters
Butter	1 cup/ 16 tablespoons/ 2 sticks	8 ounces	230 grams
Cheese, shredded	1 cup	4 ounces	110 grams
Cream cheese	1 tablespoon	0.5 ounce	14.5 grams
Cornstarch	1 tablespoon	0.3 ounce	8 grams
Flour, all-purpose	1 cup/1 tablespoon	4.5 ounces/0.3 ounce	125 grams/8 grams
Flour, whole wheat	1 cup	4 ounces	120 grams
Fruit, dried	1 cup	4 ounces	120 grams
Fruits or veggies, chopped	1 cup	5 to 7 ounces	145 to 200 grams
Fruits or veggies, pureed	1 cup	8.5 ounces	245 grams
Honey, maple syrup, or corn syrup	1 tablespoon	0.75 ounce	20 grams
Liquids: cream, milk, water, or juice	1 cup	8 fluid ounces	240 milliliters
Oats	1 cup	5.5 ounces	150 grams
Salt	1 teaspoon	0.2 ounce	6 grams
Spices: cinnamon, cloves, ginger, or nutmeg (ground)	1 teaspoon	0.2 ounce	5 milliliters
Sugar, brown, firmly packed	1 cup	7 ounces	200 grams
Sugar, white	1 cup/1 tablespoon	7 ounces/0.5 ounce	200 grams/12.5 grams
Vanilla extract	1 teaspoon	0.2 ounce	4 grams

Index

Acknowledgments

TO DIDIER, FOR EVERYTHING THAT MAKES ME LOVE WORKING WITH YOU!
TO EMELINE, THANK YOU FOR MANAGING THIS PROJECT THE WAY YOU
HAVE, WITHOUT EVER LOSING YOUR PATIENCE OR YOUR SMILE.
THANK YOU TO THE PHOTOGRAPHER, STYLIST, GRAPHIC DESIGNER, AND
THE REST OF THE TEAM AT SOLAR WHO WORKED BEHIND THE SCENES—
WITHOUT YOU, THIS BOOK WOULD NOT EXIST!
SPECIAL THANKS TO JULIA PHILIPPS FOR THE ABSOLUTELY MAGICAL COVERS
SHE CREATES! WHAT A GREAT PRIVILEGE TO SEE THEM ON MY BOOKS!
TO MY FAMILY AND FRIENDS . . .

Published originally under the title "Desserts de princesses (et de princes aussi)"
© 2019 Editions Solar, an imprint of Edi8, Paris
English translation copyright: © 2020 by Skyhorse Publishing, Inc.

Skyhorse Publishing books may be purchased in bulk at special discounts for sales promotion, corporate gifts, fund-raising, or educational purposes. Special editions can also be created to specifications. For details, contact the Special Sales Department, Skyhorse Publishing, 307 West 36th Street, 11th Floor, New York, NY 10018 or info@skyhorsepublishing.com.

Skyhorse® and Skyhorse Publishing® are registered trademarks of Skyhorse Publishing, Inc.®, a Delaware corporation.

Visit our website at www.skyhorsepublishing.com.

10 9 8 7 6 5 4 3 2

Library of Congress Cataloging-in-Publication Data is available on file.

Cover design by Kai Texel

Print ISBN: 978-1-5107-6129-2
Ebook ISBN: 978-1-5107-6130-8

Printed in China